Moving in purpose, on purpose

Moving in purpose, on purpose

The assignment, a journey of faith into the unknown

Reginald Lewis

Published by Spines
ISBN: 979-8-89383-872-5

Contents

I would like to take this time to dedicate this book to my mother, Mayetta Johnson, who throughout my life has been my #1 fan.

You have always supported my goals, aspirations, and dreams with a faith and belief in me that never failed to encourage and inspire.

Thank you for all the motherly wisdom, biblical advice and teachings that cultivated my process of growth and brought me through the journey of my life closer to God.

Your direction has paved the way to my success, thank you.

I LOVE YOU.

The 1st dream, how it all began

As the realm of night vision invaded my evening, I found myself standing confused in the middle of what seemed to be a massive highway or road, and with me stood thousands upon thousands of people appearing just as clueless as I. It was a preoccupying time of night fall the sky was dark and dreary and uncertainty filled the atmosphere with a loom of despair and anxiousness the highway seem to wind off into the distance as far as the eye could see, in-fact the only objects visible were the mass amounts of people crowding the streets, and the sky seemingly being the focal point of it all

Suddenly my attention was drawn to the dark grey dismal heavens, then out of the darkness a sound so horrifyingly in- ignorable was announced. The only thing I could think of to describe it was to in-vision 2 enormous hands almost unmeasurable in size

Piercing through the clouds grasping thousands of full grown oak trees in its clutches at each end and snapping them in half, I termed around to see what could have caused a sound of such magnitude, an unexplainable feeling of chaos, yea a stillness plundered the air , as I fixed my eyes upon the sky it was almost as If I had anticipated the happening,

Then immediately panic was birthed and confusion was born in terror. The only focus obtained was upon the faces of all the people that surrounded me, as they frantically ran past me, deep eye sockets with pupils as wide as golf balls, their cheek bones protruding expressively from their facial structure. They all ran chaotically down the wide winding road to no escape or particular destination, only to remain in their present condition and state. While looking to the heavens and attempting to evade what had initially captured their interest, the light began to shine again, and luminance once again replenished the earth and filled the atmosphere.

Based on a true dream.

Time: January 6, 2024 @ 3:40am

Morrow GA,

Jeremiah 2:10

Learn not the way of the nations, nor be dismayed by the signs of the heavens because the nations are dismayed by them.

Parental guidance

As I ponderED upon this dream placing effort into manifesting an understanding I decided to give my mother and father a call to see if some light could be shed upon this happening. Mother was immediately mentally drawn to the revealing revelation, as was my father. Though there existed a degree of correlation, there was no understanding that this vision was more of a personal retrieval of attention.

My father was so excited at such a revealing and captivating dream, He had been a student of the book of Revelation for the past 30 plus years, we talked for hours about suggestive connections, possibilities, and theological theories, however for some reason, none of the conversation seemed to assist with drawing a conclusion that led to a clearer understanding, my spirit was suggesting that there was more.

In fact, by the time it was all said and done, I was left feeling further from the truth of the matter.

This was not a message for them to decipher. It was intentionally directed at my ability and desire to know and understand this visitation. What the heavens had declared to me was for me.

Therefor I sought out the only existence that could grant an answer as well as an understanding.

I had no idea that this process would become one of often repetition, and I knew with every word, dream and sign he was drawing me closer to him, developing a more personal and intimate relationship with him, for concerning what was to come in the days ahead this would be necessary.

For God began a new work in me for a plan that had been assigned to my life since before my conception. My spirit was excited. I could feel the spirit of God moving, informing me to embrace what was coming, and so I did with all desire to please

God, however, I possessed no clue as to what I was about to endure through it all. Though it was a blissful time throughout most of the unveiling there were also times when I found myself questioning my sanity. However, the creator has a way of making his truth undeniable.

John 16:13

When the spirit of truth comes, he will guide you into all truth, for he will not speak on his own authority, but whatever he hears he will speak, and he will declare to you the things that are to come.

The second dream.

Previous to this time of dedication, sacrifice and personal time with my heavenly father, the Most High visited the world behind my eyes yet again. As I embraced the awareness of my dream state I found myself gazing upon a beautiful construct of the most brilliant landscape I had ever witnessed. As I stood there enveloped in the magnificence of a shining brook continuously filled by crystal waterfalls that sparkled like diamonds all embraced in a landscape of vegetation that was as green and vibrant as anything I had ever seen. If I had to sum it up in three words they would be (a beautiful life). It all seemed to represent life; a life full of living.

In the twinkling of an eye, I began to notice a figure appearing from the water casually strolling upon land as if it had just traveled from another world. As the divine figure reached its destination upon land, my focus was captured by a captivating sky so brilliant that it seemed to reflect the waters of the lower realm, now that I think about it (As above so below)

Captivated by the above, gazing at nothing in particular it was as if I began to brace and ready myself for something I could feel about to introduce its presence. The physical form upon arrival simply stopped in mid stride and planted his staff within the earth with such authority and stood in silence, as my eyes beheld my ears attentively stood ready to receive.

Then suddenly a resounding word from the heavens above expressed RETURN HOME! And the consciousness of the natural world invaded my existence as I awakened.

Based on a true dream!

January 13, 2024 @ 6:18am

Morrow GA,

Psalm 23:1-6

The Lord is my shepherd; I shall not want.

He maketh me to lie down in green pastures: he leadeth me beside the still waters. He restoreth my soul: he leadeth me in the path of righteousness for his name's sake.

Yea, though I walk through the valley of the shadow of death, I will fear no evil: for thou art with me; thy rod and thy staff they comfort me.

Thou preparest a table before me in the presence of mine enemies: thou anoints my head with oil; my cup runs over.

Surely goodness and mercy shall follow me all the days of my life: and I will dwell in the house of the Lord forever.

7 Days Later

IN AWE, I was simultaneously with belief and the opposing.

Exactly 7 days later I was visited yet again with instructions to return home. However, prior to this dream, I was led by the spirit in the word of God to Luke 2:1-6

Uncertain of its relevance to the parts contained within the scriptures I did notice a direct connection concerning instruction and reason, however. I could not determine a full understanding, nevertheless there was one thing I could not have been more certain of, and that was his instruction to return home.

I found myself in a state of confusion concerning the instruction considering that my birthplace had never really been considered home. Therefore, I posed myself the question, where was home?

My fondest memories had been made in Oklahoma City, probably because in that place I smiled in youth the most.

However, most of the dust raised in my life was upon the grounds of North Carolina where the hard lessons of life had been taught and learned. There my future seemed bleak, but my life's molding was wonderfully being made. But that is another part of my history for another time.

And so, I sought out the advice of my mother once again, approaching her with what seemed to be an insane inquiry: where is home for me? I asked. The only connection I really had with my homeland was my social security number.

I recall her expressing a hard but brief laugh in response to my question. She replied, boy you were born in Texas with a hint of sarcasm in her tone.

I responded that this had been known, and I proceeded to explain how it never felt as such, however regardless of this fact, this was indeed the truth.

Upon revealing the origin of the question posed she replied, seek God. And so I did.

I recall sitting in my car the very next morning at approximately 4:30am mentally preparing for work and praying for the strength, wisdom, and patience to make it through another day. I also found myself considering the events that had taken place over the last few days and while in prayer, therefore I asked God if this was indeed his plan concerning his instruction in my life and he revealed it unto me.

Amen.

As I made my way inside to punch the clock and begin my day, I was informed that we were having a meeting concerning the monthly events that had taken place. These meetings were formulated with themes, for example if a meeting took place during the super bowl the room would be decorated with corresponding décor, if it was Cinco de Myo the room would have been filled with Hispanic culture, however on this day, believe it or not the theme was traveling, The entire room was decorated as if you were making you way through an TSA area of an airport.

Immediately I was attentive especially considering I was in waiting concerning an answer from my heavenly father. At this moment it seemed as if he was tapping me on my shoulder, advising me to pay attention.

Nevertheless, as we entered the room individuals conducting the monthly meeting were handing out generic airline boarding tickets that had been printed out for a drawing that was to take place during this event.

I had not thought much about it, however as I took my seat while glancing around the room admiring how much effort had gone into making this all seem as authentic as possible I realized I was yet holding the ticket that they gave us as we entered the meeting in my hand, and so I decided to indulge in this realization. As I flipped the ticket over and positioned it right side up to better understand the contents contained upon it I instantaneously found myself in total shock, at this very moment there was no doubt in my mind that the information the I was looking upon was a personal response, a missive of instruction and divine confirmation directly from my heavenly father .

That's right, in black and yellow as clear as day. Atlanta to Dallas. Based on a true event.

January 25, 2024 @ 5am

Forest Park GA,

I was flabbergasted.

But God!

An unwelcome visitation

I had just finished editing some literature from my first book The Good Fight when the evening introduced the idea that I had reached a good stopping point for the moment, and so I decided to call it a day, announcing to my assistant who had seemed mentally preoccupied the entire time, it seemed a time to wrap things up for the evening.

As I lay peacefully in my bed resting for what I hope God would allow to be another day among the living, there was a feeling of uneasiness as if a lurking entity was present. I could feel fear creeping in and arresting my consciousness. While entertaining this presence I found myself dozing off into rest. Little did I know that it would not be a peaceful one.

As the moon took its place in the night sky slumber took its reign, my awakened state took its place in the merciful hands of God for the night.

Then suddenly my bed covering moved as if peeled back for access underneath, my eyes instantly opened with curiosity, dismissing the event I slipped back into an unconscious state, then I could feel SOMETHING positioning itself for comfortability it seemed, wrapping what felt like arms around my physical inching closer and closer until its movement awakened me.

At this point I knew I had an unwelcome visitor from the spirit world, especially considering I lived alone, I immediately leaped from my invaded resting place simultaneously clutching my Bible in midair it seemed, with no time spared I turned my sword to Psalms 91 and began reading with authority after each verse praying a prayer of binding rebuke, my determination was occupied with all vigilance to remove this unwelcome guest that decided to take residence in the wrong home. I anointed every wall, doorway, window, floor and ceiling while praying earnestly we battled all night so much so to point that by the time I finished it was 3am at which time I usually awaken to prepare for work.

With consideration to my form of employment I thought it best not to danger of myself or others. Despite the fact that I was also exhausted, I had come to the conclusion that a personal day was necessary.

Based on a true event.

February 5, 2024 @ 2am

Morrow GA,

Ephesians 6:12

We fight not against flesh and blood, but against principalities, against powers against rulers of darkness in this world, against spiritual wickedness in high places.

Note to self

PLEASE UNDERSTAND that at any point when the enemy finds out that there exists a desire to not only serve God but to live in obedience to his will, his way, and his word you have placed a spiritual target on your back, and his attention is aimed at your desire to please God. Infiltration into the plans God has for you. It is inevitable. For he knows that within the embrace of God's will is your purpose according to his plan. This alone places one in a position of victory, thereby placing a loss in the history book of the devil. However, it also positions an individual under the covering and protection of the highest. But this does not thwart the enemies advanced, for he is vigilant in them, and if we are not guarded, he will succeed in stealing and destroying your victory, your future, and your destiny for he is a master thief. It is what we do while in battle that determines the outcome of it.

That morning and the next day I noticed the spirit of God directing me in his word. Seemingly appointed scriptures pertaining to the events that had been transpiring in the past couple of days, each chapter and verse containing divine messages of instruction and revelation. God had begun a work, and this work was going to be completed.

John 10:10

The thief cometh not but to steal and to kill and to destroy. I am come that you might have life, and that they may have it more abundantly.

Divine whistle

AFTER THE BATTLE with the unwelcome visitation I found myself a bit on edge, though certain that Gods authority was dominant, it yet felt as though something was still present lurking waiting for a moment of vulnerability to attack, throughout the day my character displayed an expression of nonchalant, however the more I took notice to the nights approach the more uneasy I found myself becoming, I had already been deprived of sleep for the past few nights and I knew this could not continue., but so did my God.

Nevertheless the arrival of the evenings presence was at full bloom, I found myself in yet another battle with maintaining consciousness, the atmosphere was filled with plots of ambush, at this point I was questioning my sanity and fear had become a residing resident, however prayer was constantly upon my tongue while simultaneously attempting to display awareness, I was exhausted, this past weekend seemed to be the fight of my life, I could not recall ever being attacked with such vigilance, however my faith, and hope in the power of the creator had encouraged me so to the point of considering the fact that if I am being attacked at this level, the level of my blessing and deliverance was even greater.

As I found myself slipping into the abyss behind my eyelids I began to feel a slight breath upon my ear as if someone was attempting to whisper to me then suddenly a massively loud whistle was pronounced with such volume directly into my ear that I instantly awakened with a sharp pain striking down the side of my head. At this point I didn't know if it was the enemy torturing me or an angel waking me to avoid the enemy's attack.

I decided at this point it was time for a back-up. The only problem was is that I didn't have any.

A realization had been impressed upon my heart that I had come as far as I could go by myself.

I needed to sit in a position of stewardship and fast, at this point I understood that I needed to surround myself with individuals of a like-minded heart that contained a wisdom beyond what I presently comprehended as enough, therefore with this in mind

I knew at this point God was taking me somewhere where this would be significantly needed and added to my life, in other words this was just the beginning.

My journey consisted of so much more than I had imagined.

Not only had God instructed me on where to go, but in the mist of the attacks he was also informing me of what I would need before and along the way, as well as what needed to be implemented upon arrival. I had come to find out that all of it was very necessary in my survival for victory and purpose. I had come to understand that there was reinforcement that needed to take place as well as purification, and this was confirmed in scripture being ushered to the book of John by the spirit. Of course, in the begin I had not understood why exactly it was that I was taken to this scripture for reference until I was introduced to the true condition of my heart concerning my faith in this journey.

John 2:1-10

On the third day there was a wedding in Cana of Galilee, and the mother of Jesus was there. Now both Jesus and His disciples were invited to the wedding. And when they ran out of wine, the mother of Jesus said to Him, "They have no wine." Jesus said to her,

"Woman, what does your concern have to do with Me? My hour has not yet come."

His mother said to the servants, "Whatever He says to you, do it." Now there were set there six waterpots of stone, according to the manner of purification of the Jews, containing twenty or thirty gallons apiece. Jesus said to them, "Fill the waterpots with water." And they filled them up to the brim. And He said to them, "Draw some out now, and take it to the master of the feast." And they took it. When the master of the feast had tasted the water that was made wine and did not know where it came from (but the servants who had drawn the water knew), the master of the feast called the bridegroom. And he said to him, "Every man at the beginning sets out the good wine, and when the guests have well drunk, then the inferior. You have kept the good wine until now!"

Patience in waiting

Patience is defined as a noun and is, "the capacity to accept or tolerate delays, trouble, or suffering without getting angry or upset."

While waiting is defined as a noun it is also the act of staying in one place or remaining inactive in expectation of something. Therefore with this in mind we can conclude that patience in waiting is the HOW, the reason or purpose of the WHY.

Case in point:

Upon being instructed to return home via dream, and deciding to be obedient to the divine instructions, and remain within the will of God, I immediately began preparing for the process as also instructed.

When it was learned that the wine for the feast was depleted worry, frustration, confusion and doubt began to set in. However, Jesus' mother knew that not only did her son have the answer, but also that he was indeed the answer, therefore she instructed the servants to do as Jesus had commanded.

Jesus at this time instructed the servants of the feast to go and fill the water pots with water, in other words, go and prepare these vessels for a miracle, fill the vessels with a pure substance (WATER) and return them back to me that I may make that substance into something better and new.

Of course, many of us know the miracle performed. Jesus Christ turned the water into wine, and the masters of the banquet had never tasted anything more sweet nor satisfying. Their emotions were filled with curiosity, pleasure and yet a hint of disbelief, for they knew not of the miracle performed, only its results.

This was the message I received from my spirit throughout this process. Not only was I instructed to prepare for the miracle God was about to perform in my life, not only had he informed me of the condition of self that must be prepared for change, but my enemies and or nay sayers would not even be able to understand how I became an overcomer they would only be witnesses of the result, viewers at the table being prepared for me, and only I would be the partaker of this great feast., and know the origin of the miracle.

However, for this to be made so, I had to be as the servants that Mary instructed me to do as Jesus had commanded, for the miracle was contained within the obedience of the servant.

The following of instruction brought forth transformation, however this was no ordinary transformation, for the Bible never stated that Jesus changed the

Substance/water: it only read that he instructed them to fill the pots with water then to draw it out and take it unto the governor of the feast.

However, none of this had taken place before the process of purification. The substance would have no effect without first being purified. This is why it would be unwise, and unjust to place new wine into old skins.

Therefore considering God's desire to do a new, miraculous, and wonderful work in my life I now understood that I needed to be purified and filled so that my substance would be seen and proven by those who might attend the event that is my life as a part of my destiny, knowing that after tasting what God has blessed is confirmed by those with no idea of the work performed, that it was and is indeed good.

Questioning the process

I MUST HUMBLY ADMIT that there were times when doubt, frustration, and disbelief were present.

And most nights fighting mental battles to retain a desire for resiliency and even sanity at times it seems.

Of course, I was convicted in these times however the desire to overcome always manifested itself greater. I would express that I had no idea of how I continuously greeted victory, but then I believe this would place me as close to blasphemy as I could get without actually committing such an act, for this would strip God of the glory that he indeed deserved from me, concerning his grace, mercy and favor. I have come to understand that there is a thin line between the reality of the natural man, and wisely manifesting the abilities of the spirit man.

Often times the logic of a situation can appear obvious, however when it comes to displaying obedience, divine revelation can make the logical stand questionable, for no man according to the word of God knows the mind of God.

Nevertheless, I question, I hesitate and wonder concerning the outcome if I simply apply my 2 cents. I understand there is a work that I must labor in the meantime, as well as a stillness that must be displayed, however I am certain my labor has been designed, however that design must be respected and obeyed, not to interfere with God's perfect plan. There is his plan and my work, and if my work is not aligned with his plan, then my work is no longer the business of my Heavenly Father, but that of my own personal desires, unguided by perfection that usually concludes in regret, and the lengthening of the arrival of the miracles and blessings of God.

James 1:4-8

But let patience have her perfect work, that ye may be perfect and entire, wanting nothing.

If any of you lack wisdom, let him ask of God, who giveth to all men liberally, and upbraideth not; and it shall be given to him.

But let him ask in faith, nothing wavering. For he that wavers like a wave of the sea is driven by the wind and tossed.

For let not that man think that he shall receive anything from the Lord. A double-minded man is unstable in all his ways.

Misusing Faith

THOUGH I HAVE YET to grasp and obtain an understanding concerning my heavenly father's instructions I remain encouraged for the feeling of elevation seems nearby. However, at times it does appear to be that God does indeed possess a sense of humor, for the joy of the Lord is my strength.

Just when it seems I have it all figured out, moments of epiphany reveal otherwise, and I realize that the only conclusion reached was one that would inform me that the only thing I had figured out is that I had nothing figured out, and in these moments that one would usually find disappointment in, I discover humor, and a relief of divinely odd joy fills my atmosphere replacing frustration, curiosity and confusion with peace and comfort repositioning me to an impression of the beginning of the assignment. Though the air of peace had taken residence in my present I couldn't help but wonder if I had advanced forward closer to what the most high had in store for me, or had I retracted further from the manifestation of his blessing. I must admit there are times when it feels as though my cries for his assistance are considered a possible nuisance within my thoughts, however then the realization of his grace being sufficient invades my understanding, and once again I am replaced in a particular positioning of the process

One would believe that there are many moving parts within an assignment once it is imputed, however, there is only one true independent working part. However, make no mistake, you have a part to play, nevertheless keep in mind he is the wheel in the middle of the wheel.

I recall finishing up my workload for the day and heading back to document the events of the day's operations I found myself upon that o so familiar battle ground referred to as my mind, revisiting all the details I could recall concerning this life changing instruction that was destined to I believe reveal what I presently longed for. I found myself at a point that questioned every action that I had submitted to the situation. I was the one that had to first place myself in a position to hear, then review his word, not to mention the amount of faith that had to be applied, then act upon his word, which consisted of requesting a transfer through my employer that unveiled numerous sets of applications that were a necessary feat to hurdle. Then there was the task of finding residence in a place that I could consider perfectly situated between my job, family and place of worship, not to mention affordable. Then there was the reality of my present leasing contract, then of course there was

The whole rental vehicle, trailer, the act of moving itself, the traveling all only to rein act it all again upon arrival to the destination, after considering all of this I remember mentally inquiring of myself, platonically I might add,

If I am doing all of this, what is God going to do?

And all I remember is him responding as clearly as your voice reading these words.

"I TOLD YOU TO GO!" That's what I did.

Say less father.

Instantaneously I understood his response. Even though I had no clue of what matters he may have cleared, situations he had adjusted or snares he defeated prior to even considering visiting me in the night via dream, I had to make a move through obedience by an act of faith.

I am most certain our comparisons concerning the work I had to perform and his work would not even be close in measure. At this point foreignness is all I can ask for.

Faith if misused incorrectly, will drive one mad if allowed.

I know what you are thinking. How can faith be used incorrectly?

Well, at the time I had not realized it, but after all the signs, dreams, and scriptures revealed concerning God's instructions a decision to accept and follow his plan was obtained, or at least I thought.

I found myself faced with a situation that placed me between a rock and a hard place. Though the instructions to return home were clear it seemed I was always in need of instructions concerning what should be done first, and then what should be done next, as well as what I should do upon arrival. I desired for God to hold my hand throughout the entire process though excited and grateful that my life and its journey was yet beginning and being considered by God, deeply within I desired him to do the leg work considering it was his plan, but that's not how it works, and this I knew, nevertheless this was the selfish characteristics of an immature believer, I believed he could do it, and so I thought that he should, but why was this not a trait I could view in myself? Nevertheless, the reality of(the rock position) was that I was past due for submitting my 60 day notice to either renew my lease or terminate my lease, therefor I was liable for a $2000 fee for failure to provide this information, (the hard place) was everything else that was contingent upon this.

It had already been approximately 2 weeks since I submitted my application for transfer, and 1 since my interview. Therefore, at this point you can imagine my anxiety. With this in mind I previously fought with the process of stalling on my lease until I heard from my potential employer, without realizing I had already made up in my mind that if I was not awarded the opportunity to transition, I was simply going to renew my lease, thereby remaining rather than exhibiting obedience. Of course my plan was not God's plan and so I found my back against the wall, and that wall forced me to terminate my lease before even hearing from my potential employer. With no contact from my potential employer, no future residence to call home, unsure of my financial ability to even make the journey I terminated my lease. At this point with approximately 30 days left it finally hit me. Not only was I operating in the natural attempting to do it my way, but I was also covertly trying to overcome these obstacles without implementing my walk of faith, without trusting my Heavenly Father. Upon arrival to this realization accountability had introduced itself and the true journey of faith began.

I can now say that I have sincerely come to understand the meaning of faith without works is dead, for this is how faith is used incorrectly.

How do we know when our faith is being used incorrectly? It causes death.

John 10:10

I have come that you may have.

Life, and have it more abundantly.

Approved

THE PROCESS CONTINUES

As I lay in bed winding down from a productive day's work, I found myself heavily pondering future possibilities, strategies and conclusions. The mere considerations brought my thoughts to a boil. Just when it seemed the pressure had achieved its maximum limits my phone announces that someone is attempting to make contact. Mr Lewis? Speaking, congratulations I just wanted to inform you that we have decided to move forward with your transfer for employment with us here in Dallas, how soon would you be able to begin?

And that was that.

My heart rejoiced shamefully nevertheless it rejoiced, however though frustration discouragement and a degree of anxiety had taken residence within I sincerely found that I could not rejoice whole heartily because of this, and so I found myself repenting before celebrating unable to embrace his blessing in the manner I know my Heavenly Father desired for me to do so, I found conviction in his open door instead of a blissful greeting., nevertheless I began to realize this was yet his grace and mercy displayed.

This is why we must hold fast in the professing of our faith, for if we cannot find delight in the blessings of God, then we can never be truly satisfied with his mercies, and if we can still find joy without conviction in situations such as this then we do not deserve satisfaction nor an open door for that matter.

Nevertheless, he is continually doing great things whether we are deserving or not for he knows our begging from our end, he knows the plans he has for our lives, therefor to believe in him is to believe in his plan and purpose.

We cannot have one without the other. Should we not thank the builder for a place our hearts can find rest? For the sanctuary he provided. For the cover he raised. For the foundation that was laid with a design that held our desires in mind. He placed our desires, hopes, and passions in his blueprint because he knew what he wanted to create before he began the process of our creation for it was indeed premeditated, for he stated before he even began molding us from the dust of the earth "let us make man in our own image" this alone should be reward enough, he breathed his breath of life into our existence, therefore why does it seem impossible for our very breath to speak his name? YAHWEH

And so, in our trials, our seasons of discomfort, in the presence of emotional anxieties I encourage you to remember to breathe, breathe in peace, and a hope that his will and purpose has been implemented into the threading of your life, but most of all

Breathe in the fact of knowing that victory has been promised and so we should rest assured that it is and has been inevitably approved.

His plan vs. Our plan

I would like to begin by posing a question, how do we make plans that do not interfere with Gods plans and exercise the necessity of implementing actions within hours while remaining in the guidelines of Gods prerequisites?

Usually, our plans consist of an effort that is manifested from the natural, while God's plans are always birthed in the spirit. To walk by faith and not by sight is to walk in the spirit. When we choose to walk in the spirit we have made a conscious decision to walk by faith and trust in the word of God.

The instruction and guidance of the spirit will supersede the path of the natural and its process for this is when the divine heavenly wisdom of Zion will occupy control and lead the individual in all truth. However, one must be in line with the law and the truth of the scriptures. These must be accepted from within the heart with all sincerity. Acknowledgement must be expressed that his plan, his will, and his purpose, is not only the way, but that it is the only way.

As I sat in my car one morning approximately 2 hours early for work it felt as if I was at the end of my rope as if I could not stand another trial, test, or advance of the enemy, ready to throw in the towel and it was as if God threw it back and said wipe your tears. You may be feeling as though you are in the wilderness and that you are being attacked from all sides but I am with you. There is nothing that you are experiencing in your life that I am not between you and the issue. I am yet to lead you and as long as you proceed to know and trust me I will bring you out. All week I had been under attack and each day was coming forth appearing more stressful than the prior occurrence. I could not bring myself to understand HOW? After the reading the fasting the prayer the worship the faithfulness the obedience, how could I be going through all these discouraging trials WHY? But what we must understand is that our walk with Christ does not make us exempt from the attacks of the enemy nor the trails of life. In fact it is impossible that man should live without offense, but now unto him that is able to keep us from falling and to present us faultless before the presence of his glory with exceeding joy. To the only wise God our savior be glory and majesty dominion and power now and forever. Amen.

Jeremiah 29:11

"For I know the plans I have for you," declares the LORD, "plans to prosper you and not to harm you, plans to give you hope and a future."

Financing my obedience

I HAD no clue concerning how I was going to finance my act of obedience. I only knew that my heart desired to do so. God said go, so I began moving in the direction of his instructions.

I must admit at times we did not see eye to eye on his process but how could I contend or debate with an entity whose throne was positioned in the heavens and the earth was his footstool.

Nevertheless, I proceeded with a now transparent understanding of my faith. I had come to realize that my growth in Christ had manifested itself within me. I began to take notice concerning different responses to various situations arising throughout this process.

7-14 days is what I was informed of concerning the arrival of a loan I had taken out of my 401k to assist in financial contribution, however 30 plus days had passed not to mention the many phone calls to customer service that amounted to absolutely no avail.

However, finally after numerous attempts at rectifying this situation, there remained only one choice: cancel the first request, submit another and wait possibly another 10-14 days or potentially more. This time frame would place the arrival of said funds at the last minute, practically the day of, unless time proves gracious.

I am sure time will reveal, nevertheless, this does not halt situations from arising. As I was leaving for work one morning, I began to hear a worrisome vibration from the rear center of my car when turning. I am no mechanic however I have worked on enough vehicles to know this was my drive shaft screaming for attention, and usually when

If your vehicle desires your attention it also desires your money, so now there is the rental vehicle not to mention the trailer to haul my car, the maintenance on the car which seemingly has my dashboard lighting up like time square, then, there are the remaining bills of the present residence as well as the future bills for the new residence, the negative sign in front of the dollar amount on my bank statement, and even the current health of my baby girl Belle my staffers terroir, fortunately, but unfortunately it's a bitter sweet situation all things considered, and believe me these are just a few of the discrepancies that without hesitation or complexity come to mind.

As I sat in my truck preparing to do a pre-trip inspection before beginning my route for the day a fellow coworker approached me with an inquiry concerning our yearly reviews consisting of our bonuses and raises. The conversation revealed that our raises for starters would not be what we had expected and had been affected

Considerably by career slump due to company transitions, from external construction on the physical structure to alterations in positions at the top of the chain, nevertheless we all know poop floats downstream, and as for bonuses, well let's just say it looks most likely to be able to cover taxes as opposed to the normal x2 compensation we receive, therefor nothing was adding up including my paycheck, not to mention our hours on the clock appeared no longer plural, figuratively speaking, as I write these words I literally have to laugh, not to keep from crying, but because despite all of this I know God is able, there exists no coincidence within these sudden misfortunes, though at times life naturally just happens, however there is no doubt within my mind that my Heavenly Father has it all under control.

Literally two days remain at my current place of employment and five before the journey begins, they say time is of the essence, nevertheless I fully understand that the supreme architect of all existence is not subject to it, though it may look like crunch time, my faith yet remains unshaken, honestly I am not even certain as to how, I simply hold on and proceed in faith, truth be told it's all that I have, my faith in his word.

This is my evidence, and the fact that the entire process of following his instructions, all will be approved according to his plan and purpose for my life.

Hebrews 11:1

Now faith is the substance of things hoped for, the evidence of things not seen.

Where am I weak?

I ᴋɴᴏᴡ it may seem as though throughout these pages that there were instructions awarded, then all hell breaks loose, well, as bitter sweet as it may appear this is indeed part of the process, however I do not find it unfortunate, for it has been written, that not only do the trials of our faith work for our patients, but that they also come to make us stronger. It is what it will be.

For I heard it stated that it is impossible for man to live without offense. The enemy wasted no time in seeking the destruction of the completion of this assignment. Yes, it does feel as though all hell broke free nevertheless I take this as a compliment, for I am certain the enemy knows what the most high has in store for me, otherwise I could not believe that I would have been considered by him with so much effort. With now 3 days remaining before heading out on this new beginning I found myself in yet another struggle to believe that my Heavenly Father was going to come through for me concerning the finances that have yet to arrive via mail. This situation had been a thorn in my side the entire process, the way I previewed the outcome of these finances arriving at a particular time would begin a domino effect of catastrophe's that would start hear in Atlanta Georgia and topple every victory that had seemingly been won stretching to Dallas Texas.

The closer I became to the appointed time the more frustrated I became, I just could not bring myself to trust that God would come through, I fought, and fought to force my faith to rise to the occasion however it would not move, I attempted to focus on

The prior signs wonders and miracles that had been manifested as stated upon the previous pages of this book, though they fed my spirit, their effect had seemed to dissipate, with all that made me who I am I desired more than anything to find the faith I needed to please God in this matter, nevertheless it was at this point that I realized how feeble and fragile my faith truly was.

2 Corinthians 12:9-11

New international version

But he said to me, "My grace is sufficient for you, for my power is made perfect in weakness." Therefore, I will boast even more gladly about my weaknesses, so that Christ's power may rest on me. 10 That is why, for Christ's sake, I delight in weaknesses, in insults, in hardships, in persecutions, in difficulties. For when I am weak, then I am strong.

Moving day

THE BIG DAY had finally arrived, and this was a day out of the fiery pits or so it seemed. After a full day of finishing up with packing that started around approximately 7am, completing the reservation to pick up the moving truck at 10am, then loading the truck and cleaning the now former residence, the day had been completed around 7pm. I was exhausted, however now it was time to rest for the journey. Of course, I am sure you can probably predict that no sleep visited me that evening. I was tired and wired, and this is a bad combination considering I had 950 miles ahead of me to drive. 12am was the intended time of departure. I believe the rest finally arrived a bit after 11:30, and I found myself returning to consciousness approximately an hour and a half later. I sprang into action immediately noticing I was already behind schedule. I finished loading the remainder of the small items needed for the sleep I didn't get, cosmetics, cleaning equipment etc..... Belle my staff terrier had been terrorizing a friend for the past year, so I had to drive to pick her up before heading out, and at 2am in the morning this was a reunion for the books. If you have any idea what zoomies are please understand that this phrase would be an understatement at 2am in the morning considering my baby girl had not seen me in approximately 6 months. Nevertheless, after getting her situated in the cab of the truck the size of a moving box for about 30 minutes, we were ready to hit the highway. As we merged onto 20 west in our mobile cocoon for the next 10 hours, it began raining so hard that visibility had slowed our departure down to about 40 MPH, turning our approximate 10-hour travel into 12 easy. As I watched belle chase the raindrops on her window in excitement, I couldn't help but think this was my heavenly father's way of washing off the old cleansing and preparing us for the arrival into new.

Isaiah 43:19

See, I am doing a new thing! Now it springs up; do you not perceive it? I am making a way in the wilderness and streams in the wasteland.

2 Corinthians 5:17

Therefore, if anyone is in Christ, the new creation has come: The old has gone, and the new is here!

To be continued

Related Scriptures

- Jeremiah 2:10
- John 3:13
- Psalm 23:1-6
- Ephesians 6:12
- John 10:10John 2:1-10
- James 1:4-8
- Jeremiah 29:11
- Hebrews 11:1
- 2nd Corinthians 12:9-11
- Isiah 43:19
- 2nd Corinthian 5:17

www.ingramcontent.com/pod-product-compliance
Lightning Source LLC
Chambersburg PA
CBHW060219170726
48004CB00014B/777